Taylor Swift

AMERICAN GIRL

sona
BOOKS

sona BOOKS

© Danann Media Publishing Limited 2022

First published in the UK 2022 by Sona Books an imprint of Danann Media Publishing Ltd.

CAT NO: SON0540

Photography courtesy of

Getty images:

- Kevin Mazur
- Dave Hoga
- Rob Verhorst/Redferns
- Sandra Mu
- Christopher Polk/Billboards2012
- Christopher Polk/TAS
- Kevork Djansezian
- Dimitrios Kambouris/LP5
- Sascha Schuermann
- John Medina

- Kevin Winter
- John Medina
- Valerie Macon/AFP
- Jun Sato/GC Images
- Ethan Miller
- Jeff Kravitz/FilmMagic
- Michael Buckner
- Emma McIntyre/AMA2019
- Rick Diamond/WireImage
- TAS Rights Management 2020

- Rich Fury
- Robert Gauthier/Los Angeles Times
- Taylor Hill/FilmMagic
- John Shearer/AMA2019
- Attitude Magazine
- Alliance for Women in Media Foundation
- ANGELA WEISS/AFP
- Raymond Hall/GC
- Mark Metcalfe/TAS
- Andreas Rentz

Alamy images:
- WENN Rights Ltd
- Album

Other images Wiki Commons

Book layout & design Darren Grice at Ctrl-d

Made in Malaysia

ISBN: 978-1-915343-02-4

Contents

Me!

What's in a name? When Scott and Andrea Swift named their baby girl Taylor, after their favourite singer James Taylor, did they perhaps have a sense she would grow up to be a superstar?

The story goes that when the couple had their baby girl on 13 December 1989, their decision to name her Taylor Alison Swift was because they liked the idea of giving their daughter a name which was gender-neutral, believing it would serve her well for a future career in business. Both her parents were successful financiers, Scott had his own investment banking operation linked to Merrill Lynch and Andrea was marketing manager for an investment fund. Both imagined their daughter might follow in their footsteps and as a child Taylor herself thought the same. 'I didn't know what a stockbroker was when I was eight, but I would just tell everybody that's what I was going to be," she said, during an online Q&A session

In the event words, rather than numbers, took her on a more creative path, which has seen her enjoy more fame and success than any average financier. She has also gone on to eclipse her namesake by clocking up even more record sales and Grammy awards than multi-award winner James Taylor ever did. Her name turned out to be a fortuitous choice after all — although not in the way her parents had first imagined. 'Taylor Swift' sounded starry and memorable enough to have been specially crafted by a team of music industry experts as being perfect for a pop star.

So she had a good name — what next? Let's be clear, Taylor would be nowhere without her innate talent. But she certainly had an upbringing which helped her to make the most of it.

Taylor spent the first years of her life on the idyllic-sounding Christmas Tree Farm in West Reading, Pennsylvania in the north-east of America with her younger brother Austin. Her well-off parents had bought the 11-acre farm after her father Scott came across it as an investment opportunity. As a young girl, Taylor had the run of the place and revelled in having the opportunity to enjoy the space and nature of those woodlands, crediting her time there with helping to stoke her vivid and creative imagination.

Her parents were, and still are, the strongest guiding force in her life. She has described Scott as being 'brilliant' business-wise, but also as a doting dad, 'just a big teddy bear who tells me everything I do is perfect.'

Andrea gave up her job and devoted herself to working as a full-time mother and homemaker after Austin was born in 1993. "She raised me to be logical and practical,' Taylor said in an interview with CMT (Country Music Television). 'I was brought up with such a strong woman in my life and I think that had a lot to do with me not wanting to do anything halfway.'

Taylor also appears to have inherited some useful genes from her mother's side of the family. Andrea's mother, Marjorie Finlay, was a professional opera singer who as well as having a great voice and a flair for performance also shared some other important character traits with her granddaughter. 'Taylor has the same grace and physique of Andrea's mother,' Scott believes. 'The two of them had some sort of magic where they could walk into a room and remember everyone's name.'

Taylor remembers her grandmother as being extremely charming and 'different' to everyone else. She wanted to be like her — after all charisma and difference are useful qualities for success. But when children are young it's much easier to follow the crowd and be the same as everyone else.

So being 'different', caused problems for Taylor during her younger years and she remembers being quite a loner at school.

By the time she was at school the family had moved to the more suburban area of Wyomissing in Pennsylvania, where Taylor attended the Wyomissing Area Junior and Senior High Schools. While generally a confident person, she was self-conscious about her height — tall for her age, she found it hard to approach a group of girls who were all a head shorter than she was. Taylor's very comfortable and privileged background (including a luxurious six-bedroom house with pool and a second gorgeous holiday home in New Jersey) may also have caused others to feel jealous of her. There was also her love of country music which was unusual for a girl of her age.

Whatever the problem was, Taylor has spoken about being short of friends as a child, saying that when she was around 13 her mother was her only friend. 'I couldn't understand why my friends were being so mean to me. She [Andrea] would just take me on these adventures and we would drive around and go to towns we'd never seen before.

'Those adventures and those days of just running away from my problems—you're not supposed to run away from your problems, but when you're 13 and your friends won't talk to you and they move when you sit down at the lunch table, and your mom lets you run from those problems, I think it's a good thing... My mom was my escape in a lot of ways.'

Andrea also remembers those days, telling Elle Girl that Taylor's friendship issues got so bad at one time that she'd have to 'pick [Taylor] up off the floor'.

But despite the friendship issues, Taylor worked hard at school. Her way with words and flair for storytelling which would come to serve her well as a song writer, was already clear, so she did particularly well in her English classes.

In her spare time Taylor loved to write poems and she even ambitiously started a novel. Her other love was musical theatre. She had been a member of the Berks County Theater Association since she was 10 and here her height had proved advantageous in winning her some lead roles. She was so successful that she took extracurricular singing and acting lessons and even auditioned for some Broadway shows in New York.

Yet bubbling away beneath all this activity was her growing love for country music. It certainly didn't come from her parents — Andrea was reportedly more of a hard rock fan — yet when Taylor first heard country music she felt the music and lyrics of those songs spoke directly to her. Taylor was only six when she discovered the music of LeAnn Rimes — a teenage country star at the time — and was inspired by her performances.

As she grew up Taylor did appreciate pop music, but she could never deny her first love was country and she was a big fan of Faith Hill, Shania Twain and the Dixie Chicks. Speaking years later Taylor credited each one of these female acts with inspiring her career. 'I saw that Shania Twain brought this independence, this crossover appeal; I saw that Faith Hill brought this classic, old-school glamour and beauty and grace, and I saw that the Dixie Chicks brought this complete "We don't care what you think" quirkiness.

'I loved what all of these women were able to do and what they were able to bring to country music.'

She began to feel more and more strongly that making country music was what she wanted to do. Her ambition was given a further boost when she was performing her musical theatre roles and discovered that her voice was particularly suited to singing country music.

Realising that she needed more opportunities to practice and perform, Taylor started entering karaoke competitions. She became a familiar face at the weekly karaoke nights at the popular Pat Garrett Roadhouse in Strausstown, about 20 miles from her home. 'Never in my wildest dreams did I think she would become "Queen of the World" you know?' Roadhouse owner Pat Garrett told the BBC's Profile programme. 'She was always tidy and had a nice outfit on and looked like she was ready for show business if you know what I mean. I think she was planning this ever since she's been five years old or something.

'She had a notebook, one of those ring notebooks that you use for school, and in that notebook there was nothing but her signature. She was practicing her autograph'.

Taylor took every opportunity to perform at other venues as well and was always popular. She took extra-curricular lessons in singing, acting and playing guitar. When she was aged around 12, she saw a 12-string guitar — that's twice the number on a regular instrument which consequently makes it harder to play. Thinking it was a 'cool' instrument she asked her parents if she could have one. 'Of course, we immediately said, 'Oh no, absolutely not, your fingers are too small,' Andrea recalled in an interview with *Entertainment Weekly*. 'Not till you're much older will you be able to play the 12-string guitar'.

'Well, that was all it took. Don't ever say never or can't do to Taylor. She started playing it four hours a day — six on the weekends. She would get calluses on her fingers, and they would crack and bleed, and we would tape them up and she'd just keep on playing. That's all she played, till a couple of years later, which was the first time she ever picked up a six-string guitar. And when she did, it was like, "wow, this is really easy!"'

A local musician Ronnie Cremer gave her some lessons and helped with her first attempts at song writing.

Although her parents had the necessary funds to buy guitars and pay for extra-curricular lessons, along with the business acumen to help their daughter fulfil her dreams, they were far from 'stage parents'. At this point they still regarded her love of country music as more of a hobby and they would have encouraged and helped Taylor in whatever area she had chosen. The whole family has always pushed back against any suggestions that Scott and Andrea were fame-hungry while Taylor was their talented puppet. Although her parent's money and connections helped her along the way, Taylor had talent, ambition and drive which was all her own.

Having won the chance to open a concert for country music legend Charlie Daniels as part of a karaoke prize, Taylor became keener than ever before to find opportunities to perform. She began to realise that it was no harder for her to sing before a large crowd than the smaller ones she'd been used to in the karaoke clubs. So she began to search for bigger opportunities and came up with a genius idea of offering to sing the Star-Spangled Banner — the US national anthem — at sporting events. Her local minor league baseball team the Reading Phillies were the first to take her up on the offer. From there Taylor decided the sky was the limit. As she told *Rolling Stone* magazine years later, 'I figured out that if you could sing that one song, you could get in front of 20,000 people without even having a record deal. So, I started singing the National Anthem anywhere I possibly could ......I would just send my tapes out everywhere. I would sing the national anthem at garden club meetings. I didn't care.'   Her first appearance before a large crowd came when she was 11 and sang The Star-Spangled Banner before a Philadelphia 76ers basketball game.

It was around this time that Taylor's musical theatre singing teacher Kirk Cremer, Ronnie's brother, used his links to a recording studio to help her record some of her favourite country songs on a CD. The recording and performance opportunities now coming her way — and the thrill and satisfaction she got from it all — convinced her that a career in music was something she really wanted. Her parents too began to think this interest might be rather more than a

Taylor Swift and her mother as she wins the 50th Anniversary Milestone Award for Youngest ACM Entertainer of the Year, during the 50th Academy of Country Music Awards at AT&T Stadium on April 19, 2015 in Arlington, Texas

Scott Swift, Taylor Swift and Andrea Swift arrive at Narita International Airport on May 31, 2014 in Narita, Japan

Nashville

Known as Music City USA, Nashville has been a force in the country music scene for almost a century now. It is home to the Grand Ole Opry, an institution on American radio which is still the longest-running broadcast in history.

Beginning life as the WSM Barn Dance in 1925, the *Grand Ole Opry* is a weekly concert of country music which showcases a mix of singers and musicians performing country, bluegrass, Americana, folk, and gospel music, interspersed with comedy sketches. Over the years it has launched the careers of stars such as Elvis Presley and country music legends including Dolly Parton and Garth Brooks.

As well as being home to the concert, Nashville became the natural base for the related record labels — so many opened offices in the city's downtown area that it became known as 'Music Row'. The place heaves with key movers and shakers in the country music scene.

ON THE AIR SATURDAY EVENINGS!

GRAND OLE OPRY

pastime. Their ability in marketing and money came into its own when, in 2002, they were smart and quick off the mark to make the most of the internet, still in relative infancy, by creating a MySpace page for her. They went on to secure taylorswift.com as a website address back in the mid-2000s, in the early days of the internet and social media platforms, complete with download links to some of her songs, some covers and a few of her own.

Could it be that Taylor might actually be heading somewhere with her music? Even though she was still a child it was becoming a distinct possibility. Her parents began to believe she might really have something. And no one was more certain about it than Taylor herself. It was while watching a documentary about Faith Hill, one of her favourite singers, that something of a plan came into Taylor's head. She described it as 'a little bell going off'. In the documentary, Faith talked about how she had moved to the home of country music in Nashville, Tennessee, to further her career. Taylor decided she needed to do the same. She was determined to make it. Operation 'Get me to Nashville' had begun.

Let's go to Nashville

'**H**ey, can we move to Nashville?' Taylor began asking her parents, becoming more and more insistent by the day. It seemed unlikely. The family had a great life in Pennsylvania, why would they uproot to move 700 miles and a 10-hour drive away? Lots of young girls have big dreams which they outgrow as they become teenagers but Taylor was different. She wasn't interested in partying and drinking like many of her classmates. She did use her first experiences of young love, requited or otherwise, as content for her songs, but other than that was wholly focused on her future.

She kept going... and going, explaining how the town worked and pleading with her parents to help her make her country music dreams come true. The city was full of country music, anyone who was anyone in the industry was there, record labels, song writers and managers. There were festivals, showcases and countless other opportunities. The place was, and still is, the world capital of the country scene — alive with the sound of twangy guitars, cowboy boots and sentimental ballads.

Andrea has since spoken about one of the reasons she began to take her daughter's idea of Nashville seriously. 'She never in her life ever said, 'I want to be famous' or 'I want to be rich' or 'I want to be a star.' Those words absolutely never came out of her mouth. If they had, I would have said, 'Honey, maybe you're doing it kind of for the wrong reasons.'

Taylor just wanted to be where the country action was.

In a bid to meet her daughter halfway, Andrea agreed to take Taylor on a trip to Nashville during a school holiday so that she could visit some record companies and hand deliver copies of the karaoke demo CDs she had made.

Off they went. Taylor was happy and full of hope as she visited the offices of the famous record companies lining Music Row, leaving copies of her CD at reception along with her contact details, full of expectation that she would get a call back.

But of course, these professionals were never going to take a chance on an untried 11-year-old. Plus, they were inundated with pitches from other hopeful wannabees. Taylor hadn't demonstrated anything like enough talent to make them take notice of her. She didn't

Truths about Taylor

She has pet cats called
Olivia, Meredith and Benjamin Button

She is 5ft 10ins tall

Her eyes are blue

Her brother Austin is now an actor

6'0"

5'8"

5'4"

5'0"

4'8"

Taylor & Austin Swift

stand out, other than by being so young, and even that fact was perceived as a negative. She returned home sad but wiser and undaunted, believing that she just needed to try harder to get noticed. Once again she wanted, and needed, to be different.

While she considered her next move and continued to work on persuading her parents of the possibilities on offer in Nashville, her father Scott received similar advice from karaoke bar owner Pat Garrett. One day when Scott and Pat were discussing Taylor, Pat says that he said, 'In Hershey they make bars, in Detroit they make cars, in Nashville they make stars — move to Nashville'.

As the family discussed their next move to support Taylor, events began to overtake them. The sporting occasions at which she performed were becoming increasingly prestigious, and in 2002 Taylor sang at the US Open tennis championships. Here she caught the attention of music talent manager Dan Dymtrow, who had spent time working with pop star Britney Spears. He saw similar potential in 12-year-old Taylor and agreed with her and her parents agreed that they would begin to work together.

ville

The first deal he organised was an appearance in a feature in *Vanity Fair* magazine. In a section headed 'Rising Stars' and promoted by Abercrombie & Fitch, Taylor was featured with other potential stars of the future, all wearing items from the clothing company's autumn range. It was more of a modelling assignment than a music opportunity, but Taylor was pictured with her guitar and the feature was well respected.

Taylor then began making more frequent trips to Nashville, taking part in industry showcases and managing to get the occasional meeting with a record label. Another promotional opportunity came when she was signed up to contribute one of her own songs to an album being sponsored by Maybelline, the cosmetics business.

Things were really starting to happen and eventually the buzz around Taylor paid off when she was offered a development deal by RCA which would give her sponsorship and opportunities to record. With something solid to build on at last the family took the brave decision to relocate permanently to Nashville.

Ready for it ...

So it was pastures new for the Swift family.

Merrill Lynch had an office in Nashville and Scott arranged to transfer his work there. The family bought a house in Hendersonville, Tennessee, about 15 miles outside Nashville city centre and began to set up their new lives.

Taylor enrolled at the local high school and was much happier, going on to make some good and supportive friends at last.

It was a new beginning for the whole family. Taylor appreciated the effort her parents and brother were making on her behalf but says she didn't feel stressed by it.

'I know I was the reason they were moving but they put no pressure on me,' she said in an interview with *Self* magazine. 'They were like, "Well we need a change of scenery anyway" and "I love how friendly the people in Tennessee are"'.

Andrea has also spoken about the circumstances of their relocation, telling *Entertainment Weekly* that, as a family, they were always careful never to frame the move as being about Taylor 'making it' …'Because what a horrible thing if it hadn't happened, for her to carry that kind of guilt or pressure around.

'And we moved far enough outside Nashville to where she didn't have to be going to school with producers' kids and label presidents' kids and be reminded constantly that she was struggling to make it. We've always told her that this is not about putting food on our table or making our dreams come true.'

Things went well for Taylor, just as she had hoped. She enjoyed school and made friends, including Abigail Anderson, who is still a friend today. Abigail had big dreams of her own — she was a promising swimmer who went on to win a scholarship to Kansas University — and the girls formed an immediate bond.

But most of all, Taylor loved what was happening music-wise, outside of her lessons, where, under the terms of her RCA deal, she now had the chance to work with many of the established Nashville song writers on the famous Music Row including respected names such as Troy Verges, Brett Beavers, and the Warren Brothers. It was an incredible opportunity, for anyone, but particularly a 14-year-old. Of course, Taylor knew she had lots

to prove — these songwriters were all older than she was, and she knew she needed to be at the top of her game to gain their respect. She would be out to impress, arriving ready to work, armed with some ideas for melodies, choruses and lyrics. She was in an unusual situation — schoolgirl by day, industry professional by night. But she knew that her USP was in creating her own songs, which she did by singing melodies onto her iPhone as voice memos, and writing down lyrics in the Notes section, so she was keen to hone her craft and put the hours in.

One of Taylor's earliest and most successful song writing collaborations was with established lyricist Liz Rose. The pair hit it off and Liz was impressed by Taylor's clear vision of what she wanted to say and the incredible musical 'hooks' she would conjure up.

Speaking about her work with Taylor she said she never changed much of Taylor's work, instead she helped her to improve and hone it. She's such a force,' Liz told *Rolling Stone* magazine. 'You remember the songs you write with Taylor, because the emotion that goes into them is so palpable. One of my daughters is her age, so I understood that I needed to stand back a bit and make sure we wrote Taylor songs, not Liz songs. I didn't mess with her.'

One of the first tracks the pair created was Tim McGraw, which really kicked off Taylor's career proper.

Originally this song was called *When You Think Tim McGraw.* The Tim in the title was an established country star, 20 years Taylor's senior, whose music she loved and who was married to her heroine Faith Hill. The premise of the song was that his music would always remind her of her first love in high school — a romance she knew would peter out naturally once her boyfriend, a senior, left to go to college.

The idea for the song's tune came to Taylor during a maths lesson. After she'd worked it up with some additional melodies she took it to Liz and the pair finished it together. Other early compositions with Liz were *Lucky You* and *Teardrops on My Guitar.*

Taylor's name was becoming known around Nashville. The word on the street was that she had maturity and talent way beyond her years. Despite her youth she was writing songs which were far more than mere teenage angst anthems — her themes were universal and meaningful and capable of creating powerful emotional connections with listeners. As a teenage singer-songwriter, Taylor was an anomaly in the country music industry — there had never been anyone quite like her before, able to capture a new market, young girls, and interest them in country music.

For her part, Taylor was beginning to feel constrained by the RCA deal which she believed was holding her back by leaving her languishing in the 'development stage' for a further four years when she actually felt ready to get going now.

So when Sony/ATV came calling in May 2005, offering Taylor the chance to write for some of their artists, she gladly accepted the offer and, aged 15, became the youngest staff writer they had ever employed.

Sony executive Arthur Buenahora remembers the day Taylor played some of her own compositions for him on her guitar. 'The songs were great, but it was her, really,' said Arthur. 'She was a star. She lit up the room. I liked her attitude. She was very easy to root for.'

Encouraged by the fact that other labels were coming to realise her worth, Taylor decided not to take up RCA's offer of a extending her development deal for a further year. It had served its purpose as far as she was concerned and was now more of a restraint as it didn't allow her to record her own material.

'I figured, if they didn't believe in me then, they weren't ever going to believe in me,' she said later of the RCA relationship

Walking away from RCA was brave. But the gamble paid off. Enter Scott Borchetta

Taylor Swift (R) with president of Big Machine Records Scott Borchetta (center) and Sandy Borchetta seen backstage during the 2008 CMT Awards at Curb Event Center at Belmont University on April 14, 2008 in Nashville, Tennessee

Everything has changed

Scott Borchetta was a seasoned and successful music industry executive when he came across Taylor. His 20-year career had included time with Mary Tyler Moore (MTM) records and DreamWorks Records — which also had a country music arm — but now, in search of a new challenge he was setting up a new record label of his own.

Having heard about the buzz around Taylor he decided to watch her perform in a showcase one night at Nashville's Bluebird Café. He picked up the story during a later interview with CBS. 'There were several other record companies that were in the room. And I'm looking around, I'm going, 'I hope none of these other guys are getting it.'

Because Scott had decided that Taylor would be the perfect artist for the launch of his new label. She was bright and talented with a good work ethic and a positive attitude. When he outlined his plans and shared the ideas for his independent label with Taylor and her family they were impressed and liked the idea of shaking up the established order a bit.

He called his company Big Machine Records, with Taylor Swift as his first signing. He is on record as saying he fell in love with her music

At this point Taylor stopped going to high school so she could concentrate on her music and accommodate her touring schedule. She was home-schooled for her junior and senior years, finishing the work for both in just one year and graduating a year early.

Big Machine's big first move was to launch *Tim McGraw* as Taylor's first single. Scott Borchetta ran a clever and effective campaign to get the single on to the playlists of all the country music radio stations. By now Taylor was a masterful user of MySpace which she used to promote the song and she also handwrote sweet thank you notes to the DJs who played her song. She put in some miles as well as Andrea drove her daughter around to tour radio stations.

The single got a lot of radio play over the summer of 2006, hitting number six on the

Billboard Hot Country Songs chart and number 40 on the main Billboard chart.

Meanwhile, Big Machine was working on producing Taylor's first album. Self-titled it featured Taylor's successful Tim McGraw as the lead track, along with another seven tracks she had co-written with Liz Rose and three tracks she had written by herself.

Released in October 2006, *Taylor Swift*, the album, sold 39,000 copies in its first week, but then began to grow as more of its tracks were released as singles.

With no guarantees that her album would be a success Taylor was still plugging away on the country scene. She kept up a busy schedule of performances, including taking up some brilliant opportunities to open for artists Rascal Flatts, Brad Paisley, Kenny Chesney and George Strait — named the 'King of Country' at the time.

The fact that artists of this calibre thought Taylor worthy of a slot in their shows was a huge vote of confidence in her. These performances as a support act put Taylor in front of large and discerning live audiences who really knew their country music and she went down well. For her part Taylor found that she loved sharing her music and got a massive buzz from standing in front of people who really seemed to connect with it.

Boosted by this kind of exposure, her album sales began to build.

The *Tim McGraw* single rose to #6 on *Billboard's* Hot Country Songs chart, and two other singles released from the album all made it into the top 10 of the Billboard country chart and the Top 40 of the Hot 100 pop chart in 2007: *Teardrops on My Guitar*, released in February 2007 and *Our Song*, in August 2007; *Our Song* also provided Taylor with her first #1 on the Billboard Country Chart.

Taylor Swift

Release date: October 2006 | Record label: Big Machine

TRACK LIST

1. Tim McGraw
2. Picture to Burn
3. Teardrops on My Guitar
4. A Place in This World
5. Cold As You
6. The Outside
7. Tied Together with a Smile
8. Stay Beautiful
9. Should've Said No
10. Mary's Song (Oh My My My)
11. Our Song

Taylor's eponymous debut album introduced her to the world when she was 16, the year after she signed with Big Machine Records. It went on to spend 157 weeks on the Billboard 200 chart, making it the longest-charting album of the first decade of the new millennium. The album also topped the Billboard Top Country Albums chart for 24 weeks and went on to be multi-platinum.

This collection of moody melodies about adolescent longing gave Taylor five chart hits including her breakthrough song Tim McGraw, written about the country star Tim McGraw whose songs would always remind her of a first love in high school — a relationship which she knew would end when her boyfriend, a senior, left to go to college. The single spent eight months on the Billboard country singles chart and spent two weeks at number 40 on the Billboard Hot 100 chart.

As well as proving her huge talent, these early songs gave fair warning that she was into 'relationship' themes of all types. Whether singing wistfully about doomed love, or bitterly about betrayal, Taylor is unafraid to bare and share her feelings.

The album was a big commercial success, winning the then 19-year-old Taylor a 2008 Grammy nomination for 'Best New Artist' — although she lost out to Amy Winehouse on the night.

This success brought further opportunities and recognition, including the chance to perform *Tim McGraw* at the Academy of Country Music New Artists Show in Las Vegas where she got to meet McGraw himself and his wife, Faith Hill, for the first time. The meeting was fortuitous as the couple asked Taylor to open for them on their forthcoming tour.

Then at the end of year Country Music Association Awards, Taylor picked up the fiercely contested prize for Best New Artist. Previous recipients of this CMA Horizon Award include her favourites Dixie Chicks, Carrie Underwood and Garth Brooks. Her

thank you speech charmed the audience as she thanked everyone from her family to her record company and even God. She ended with the line 'This is definitely the highlight of my senior year,' genuinely meant. Yet there was actually something more to come — a Grammy nomination as Best New Artist.

She'd barely had time to recover from the shock and joy of her Horizon award when the Grammy nomination was announced. Such validation was almost overwhelming for Taylor who celebrated her 18th birthday in December that year knowing things were starting to happen for her. Her parents threw her a huge, pink-themed party and Big Machine thanked their new star with the gift of a bright pink Chevy Silverado with her signature emblazoned on the side.

It was becoming clear that Taylor was going to break through big style.

Taylor Swift on the red carpet during 2006 CMT Music Awards, Curb Events Center at Belmont University in Nashville, Tennessee

Wildest dreams

All Taylor's dreams were beginning to come true.

Although she didn't win the Grammy — which went to Amy Winehouse — her very presence on the list was enough to catapult her into public consciousness. And plenty of other awards were heading her way. She picked up that year's Country Music Television Awards for Video of the Year and Female Video of the Year with Our Song, then won Top New Female Vocalist at the Academy of Country Music Awards ceremony in Las Vegas, where she also sang. An early signal of her flair for fashion came when she incorporated a surprise on-stage outfit change into her performance of her hit track Should've Said No. Her performance started quietly, as she sat on a stool, dressed casually in a black hoodie and jeans, playing her acoustic guitar,. Then the action started to build with the song as she got up, threw her guitar off stage and stood at the microphone as dancers arrived on stage.

The costume trick came for the second verse as dancers either side of her pulled at her outfit from either side and it came away to reveal Taylor in a much skimpier short black evening dress. Then for the song's finale Taylor walked to the back of the stage and stood under a waterfall, getting completely soaked as she belted out the end of the song. It was an arresting performance.

Chart success continued. Picture to Burn — the third single from her album had made the Country and Hot 100 charts in January, so when Should've Said No, did the same in May 2008 it made Taylor the first female artist to have five hit singles from a debut album. As well as both going platinum, these two songs served to solidify Taylor's position as 'Queen of the Break-up Anthem'. By the end of 2008, the Taylor Swift album had sold more than three million copies and proved that Taylor had cross-over appeal — a huge bonus for an artist and her burgeoning record label.

The album was released on CD and spent 20 weeks at the top of the country charts. She also passed 50 million streams of her videos on MySpace.

Big Machine built on this momentum by releasing an EP called Beautiful Eyes, exclusive to Walmart stores, which did well, with 45,000 copies sold in the first week alone and going on to make #9 on the Billboard 200 albums chart and #1 on the Top Country chart.

Quick to realise that images of Taylor would shift magazines and newspapers, the media began to take great interest in her. Taylor did some cover shots and when in late summer of 2008 she began a romance with Joe Jonas of the Jonas Brothers the media began what would be an ongoing obsession with Taylor's love life.

In late October 2008, Taylor performed the National Anthem at the World Series baseball classic, game three, in Philadelphia. She had done such performances for years, but now came an important distinction — while in the past Taylor had been the one asking to sing to get noticed, now she was being invited to sing because she had been noticed.

At the November 2008 BMI Country Awards in Nashville, *Teardrops on My Guitar*, which she had co-written, won country song of the year.

But the focus was otherwise on the highly anticipated release of Taylor's second album scheduled for November. Entitled *Fearless* it was a collection of guitar-driven songs which redefined the 'teen pop' genre. Sometimes sounding like diary entries, the songs had strong

Performing the national anthem before the Philadelphia Phillies take on the Tampa Bay Rays in game three of the 2008 MLB World Series, October 25, 2008

narratives as Taylor drew on her real-life experiences, which at that point were about issues facing teenage girls including romance and heartbreak.

'I write as life happens to me,' Taylor confirmed in an interview with *Rolling Stone* in 2010. As with her debut album, several singles were spun off *Fearless* ahead of its release. The standout track was *Love Story* which came out in September. Taylor told *Time* magazine that she wrote the song on her bedroom floor in about 20 minutes. Based on the story of Romeo and Juliet, but with a happy ending, *Love Story* became massive. In under a year, it had notched up the highest number of paid downloads in history for a country song, surpassing 3 million. It became the first country song to top the Billboard mainstream Top 40 chart and went on to sell over six million copies in the US and 18 million copies worldwide.

Love Story was also released internationally and hit the charts in several countries, including making #1 in Australia and #2 in the UK.

Fearless

Release date: November 2008 | Record label: Big Machine

TRACK LIST

1. Fearless
2. Fifteen
3. Love Story
4. Hey Stephen
5. White Horse
6. You Belong with Me
7. Breathe
8. Tell Me Why
9. You're Not Sorry
10. The Way I Loved You
11. Forever and Always
12. The Best Day
13. Change

Fearless helped Taylor to graduate from 'singer-songwriter prodigy to singer-songwriter superstar' according to respected rock critic Pierre Perone. Overall it received hugely positive reviews with other critics agreeing that Taylor had improved her song writing abilities. Many praised the honesty and vulnerability she displayed in her 'mature' lyrics.

The album debuted at #1 on the Billboard 200 chart and topped the charts for 11 non-consecutive weeks which was longer than any other album that decade. Its two most successful tracks — Love Story and You Belong with Me gained huge traction in the digital market bringing Taylor to a wider mainstream audience and helping her break out from the country music scene.

Fearless sold more than 590,000 copies in its first week, the best first-week sales for any female artist that year — and hugely satisfying for Taylor who had written seven of the tracks herself and co-written the others. It reached double-platinum in just four weeks, eventually certified Diamond by the RIAA, and was voted 2009's Album of the Year by both the Country Music Association and the Academy of Country Music. It also topped charts in Australia and Canada and has sold 12 million copies worldwide.

And of course, it would go on to win Taylor her first Grammy awards — picking up Album of the Year and Best Country Album at the 52nd Annual Grammy Awards in February 2010. The achievement made Taylor, then 20 years old, the youngest artist ever to win the award, a record she held for 10 years until 2020 when Billy Eilish won aged 18. She also won two more Grammys that night for Best Female Country Vocal Performance and Best Country Song with White Horse.

As well as breaking out of the country genre, Taylor was breaking out of North America and on her way to conquering the world.

Time to Hit the Road

In early January 2009, Taylor became the youngest musical guest — and one of the few country stars — ever to appear on the American institution that is Saturday Night Live, which was then enjoying its 32nd year on air.

However, that achievement was soon overshadowed by the big news that followed — the announcement of Taylor's first headline tour. She would play 52-cities through the US and Canada, Europe, Japan and Australia between April and September 2009. Tickets sold out in minutes. Support acts were, variously, Kellie Pickler, Gloriana and Justin Bieber with guest artists including John Mayer, Katy Perry and Faith Hill.

'Headlining my own tour is a dream come true,' Taylor told the press. This way I can play more music every night than I ever have before. Having written my own songs, they are all stories in my head, and my goal for this tour is to bring those stories to life.' Ever concerned about her fans, Taylor vowed those tickets would be 'affordable' with prices starting at $20.

All the ideas and experience she had gained while touring with other acts was put to good use as Taylor meticulously planned her Fearless tour. She was across everything from backstage to onstage, choreography to costume, lighting to imagery.

She had always enjoyed performing live and was determined to enjoy herself — which she knew would only happen if she was happy with her show. She had always set high standards for herself so the tour would be no exception. As she has told journalists many times, 'I love being onstage. It's one of my favourite things in the world.'

Fans loved what she did with her show, including moving about the venues performing in different locations throughout the evening, up close and personal with the audience. The show was on a huge scale and quite theatrical with lots of 'scenes' and costume changes. Taylor even included simulated 'rain' on stage and got drenched while singing *Should've Said No.*

There was a real youthful exuberance about her performance. Now operating on a world stage, Taylor had rubber-stamped her claims to be the next big thing in popular music.

Taylor's Truths

13 is her lucky number. She paints it on her hand before a show and so do her fans.

Speaking to MTV in 2009, she explained: 'I was born on the 13th. I turned 13 on Friday the 13th. My first album went gold in 13 weeks. My first number one song had a 13-second intro. Every time I've won an award I've been seated in either the 13th seat, the 13th row, the 13th section or row M, which is the 13th letter. Basically whenever a 13 comes up in my life, it's a good thing.'

Taylor Swift speaks onstage after Beyonce allowed her to finish her speech that was interrupted by Kanye West earlier in the showd during the 2009 MTV Video Music Awards at Radio City Music Hall on September 13, 2009 in New York City

Bad Blood

Of course as Taylor's star began to rise so did the column inches she generated. She was now an adult so suddenly the media saw her as fair game and became interested in everything about her, particularly her love life. Taylor's early romances with Joe Jonas and Taylor Lautner had been well publicised. Taylor had also moved into a penthouse apartment of her own in Nashville and was enjoying life in her first home of her own as her career went from strength to strength.

But what happened next would ensure that people who had not yet heard of her would know her name after an incident that moved her swiftly off the music pages and into the headlines — even generating comment from US President Barack Obama.

It was of course the incident with Kanye West at the 2009 MTV Video Music Awards. Then aged just 19, Taylor had won Best Female Video for her song *You Belong with Me* and was on stage making her acceptance speech when she was rudely interrupted. She had only got as far as saying 'I always dreamed about what it would be like to maybe win one of these.... ' when suddenly rapper and record producer Kanye West appeared and wrested the microphone from her, saying 'Yo, Taylor, I 'm really happy for you, I'mma let you finish, but Beyoncé' — who had been nominated for her hit *Single Ladies* — 'had one of the best videos of all time! One of the best videos of all time."

The incident completely ruined Taylor's moment of celebration and glory. It was one of her first big mainstream awards and shock and dismay was written clearly over her face as Kanye gave her back the microphone and walked offstage. Taylor was evidently at a loss as to what to do next, her mouth was open in shock, and she even seemed to sway slightly before leaving the stage herself without finishing her speech or saying another word. She and Andrea were reportedly found crying backstage afterwards. And awkwardly Taylor had yet to give her promised live performance.

.

Of course, the pro that she is, she recovered and managed to sing *You Belong with Me* in what turned out to be an epic performance. Later in the evening Beyonce was on stage to pick up an award herself and she took the opportunity to invite Taylor to join her and finish her speech. Kanye was also later shamed into apologising, some consolation, but nothing could give Taylor back the real time moment she had missed.

The event was captured by cameras and replayed endlessly on TV and online and made headlines around the world. Even the

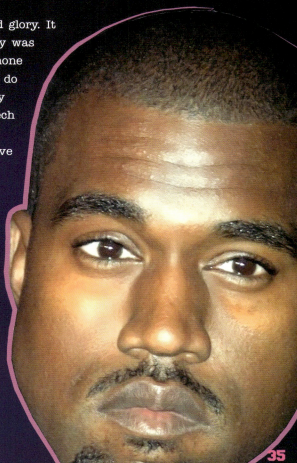

Kanye West

Katy Perry at the 52nd Annual Grammy Awards held at The Beverly Hilton Hotel on January 30, 2010, California

US President got involved, calling Kanye a 'jackass' when he was asked for his opinion.

At the time Taylor was praised for her dignified response. She has since said that the fallout was 'handled very privately,' adding, 'I think that you learn a lot of lessons as you're growing up, and one of them has to be human compassion'. As ever Taylor wrote about the experience. Her *Speak Now* album track *Innocent*, is, thought to be about Kanye where the lyrics run; "Thirty-two and still growing up now/Who you are is not what you did / You're still an innocent'.

Over the years there was some comment that the incident gave Taylor the publicity push which made her name, whereas the prize she had won that night rather proved that she was already hugely famous and respected.

Famous feuds

Over the years the 'feud' with Kanye West has rumbled on. Having seemingly resolved when Kanye attended one of Taylor's concerts with his then wife Kim Kardashian in 2015, there was further unpleasantness in 2016 when Kanye released a track called *Famous* which included a section naming Taylor and apparently referencing the incident by ending with the words 'I made that b**ch famous'.

There was naturally another furore and Kanye defended himself by saying that he had got Taylor's permission before using the line.

But Taylor's representatives dismissed that idea saying that they had not endorsed it and also cautioned Kanye about releasing a song 'with such a strong misogynistic message'.

In a rare public comment Taylor made a veiled reference to the incident, saying simply that; 'There are going to be people along the way who try to undercut your success or take credit for your accomplishments or your fame — but if you just focus on the work and you don't let those people side track you, someday when you get where you're going, you'll look around and you will know that it was you, and the people who love you, who put you there — and that will be the greatest feeling in the world.'

Katy Perry

Katy and Taylor reportedly fell out in 2014 over a row about some dancers both wanted on their upcoming tours.

Taylor said Katy had tried to sabotage her Red arena tour by trying to hire a group of people she was planning to take on the road. The song *Bad Blood* is said to have been inspired by the public feud. For her part Katy told *Rolling Stone* the former friends were now 'just straight-up enemies' and her song *Swish* is supposedly about the dispute. But all was resolved a few years later when Katy sent Taylor an actual olive branch including a note saying, 'miscommunications' and 'deeply sorry' and the pair made friends again.

Speak Now

Never one to sit back on her laurels, Taylor had also begun working on her third album Speak Now almost as soon as Fearless had been released.

The album was another triumph for Taylor who had written every track for this, her third collaboration with producer, songwriter and musician Nathan Chapman, as they experimented with the country pop style they had invented.

Speak Now marked an important point in Taylor's career by documenting her transition from adolescent to adult star. She now had completely different inspiration and included songs about real, rather than imagined, love and heartbreak.

After the album's release, Taylor embarked on her Speak Now World Tour, visiting 17 countries across Asia, Europe, North America, and Australasia between February 2011 and March 2012. Again scenery, costume and production values were high

Speak Now

Release date: October 2010 | Record label: Big Machine

TRACK LIST

1. Mine
2. Sparks Fly
3. Back to December
4. Speak Now
5. Dear John
6. Mean
7. The Story of Us
8. Never Grow Up
9. Enchanted
10. Better than Revenge
11. Innocent
12. Haunted
13. Last Kiss
14. Long Live

In its first week, Speak Now sold more than a million copies and went on to become triple platinum, making number one in the US, Canada, Australia and New Zealand, and reaching number six in the UK. Six singles were released to support the album, with Mine and Back to December making the top 10 of the Billboard Hot 100.

Taylor Swift performs on the opening night of her Speak Now tour at the LG Arena on March 23, 2011 in Birmingham, England

Taylor Swift performs on the opening night of her Speak Now tour at the LG Arena on March 23, 2011 in Birmingham, England

and theatrical, while Taylor also managed to create moments of spontaneity which enchanted audiences.

It was another massive success with critics praising everything from its sheer visual impact to Taylor's performance and connection with the audience. Many of the tracks on this album were perfect for performance in the big arenas Taylor was able to command these days.

It became the highest-grossing female and solo tour of 2011, earning over $97 million.

Taylor Swift was now a world-famous star. But why settle for that when you could become even more....

Taylor Swift performs live on stage at Ahoy in Rotterdam, Netherlands during her Speak Now World Tour on 7th March 2011

41

Taylor Swift playing a sold-out crowd of over 51,000 fans on her 'Speak Now' World Tour, Lincoln Financial Field in her home state of Pennsylvania

The final bow at Taylor Swift's 111th show on her Speak Now World Tour at Vector Arena on March 18, 2012 in Auckland, New Zealand

The Red era

Now recognised and respected as a musician, Taylor was named Woman of the Year by Billboard in 2012 — making her the youngest artist to receive that honour — listed by Forbes as the highest earning star aged under 30 and included among Billboard's Top 40 Money Makers in Music.

Alongside this serious coverage and appreciation for her talents, ran another strand of publicity around her various romances — the media was keen to pair her up. Taylor now had several high-profile relationships under her belt, including a well-publicised romance with actor Jake Gyllenhaal, and was beginning to make a name for herself for using her experiences as fodder for her music. But as the saying goes, 'write what you know'. As Taylor put it in an interview with radio station NPR; 'The first thing that I think about when I'm writing my lyrics is directly communicating with the person the song is about. I think what I've learned recently is that it's not heartbreak that inspires my songs, it's not love that inspires my songs; it's individual people that come into my life.'

When it came to creating her fourth album, *Red* in 2012 Taylor wanted something different. As she told Rolling Stone's 500 Greatest Albums of all Time podcast, 'At 22, I was already watching newer, cooler artists come out every week. I was already feeling like, 'You know.... I'm on my fourth record, what can I offer people?' That was sort of when I was like, 'No, you know what? I don't want this to be the part of me that stays in this one place musically forever and bores people to death. It was an interesting wrestling match with my own fears of remaining stagnant that made *Red* the kind of joy ride that it ended up being'.

Taylor Swift accepts the Woman of the Year award onstage at the 2012 Billboard Music Awards held at the MGM Grand Garden Arena on May 20, 2012 in Las Vegas, Nevada

This was the album which boldly stated Taylor's wish to move from country star to major league player and made her one of the most successful artists in the world. The title 'Red' is a reference to the extreme, 'red', emotions that Taylor experienced during the album's conception phase, when she described feeling 'intense love, intense frustration, jealousy, confusion …[where] there's nothing in between'.

The pop hooks in tracks such as *I Knew You Were Trouble* and *We Are Never Ever Getting Back Together* were phenomenal, while the lyrics were generally among the most insightful she had ever produced. Reflecting on the album years later, Taylor told Billboard, 'I look back on this as my true breakup album, every other album has flickers of different things. But this was an album that I wrote specifically about pure, absolute, to the core, heartbreak.'

Keen to find a new sound to expand her musical appeal, Taylor and her team brought in two Swedish producers, proven hit makers who were shaking up the mainstream charts, Max Martin and Shellback. While Big Machine still promoted the album's country credentials, and the track list included some country ballads, other tracks, and the most successful tracks, were undeniably pure pop. Critics noted Taylor's vocals had lost their country twang.

Seven singles were released to support the album, four of which made the top 10 of the US Billboard Hot 100, while the lead single *We Are Never Ever Getting Back Together* gave Taylor her first number one on the Billboard singles chart.

Taylor Swift performs onstage at the 54th Annual Grammy Awards held at Staples Center on February 12, 2012 in Los Angeles, California

Stellar single

Never Ever Getting Back Together

This upbeat pop rock tune about not getting back together with an ex quickly gained popularity and rose to number one by making one of the biggest leaps up the charts in history, moving up 72 spots in a single week to give Taylor her first number one on the Billboard Hot 100 chart.

Pinnacle Award Winner Taylor Swift speaks onstage during the 47th annual CMA awards at the Bridgestone Arena on November 6, 2013 in Nashville

The album spent seven weeks at the top of the Billboard 200 album chart, giving Taylor the accolade of being the first female artist and the second act since The Beatles to have three consecutive albums at number one for at least six weeks. It gave Taylor her first number one in the UK, while it also topped the charts in Australia, Canada and New Zealand.

Taylor promoted the album with the colossal Red Tour which ran from March 2013 to June 2014, becoming the most successful tour by a country artist of all time, grossing $150 million. It was a massive production featuring 15 dancers, four backing singers, a seven-piece band, multi-level stages, hydraulics, confetti showers and costume changes galore for Taylor.

In all, *Red* earned over 50 accolades, including four nominations at the 56th Annual *Grammy Awards*. The single *I Knew You Were Trouble* won 'Best Female Video' at the 2013 MTV Video Music Awards, while Taylor herself won 'Best Female Country Artist' at the 2012 American Music Awards and 'Artist of the Year' at the 2013 ceremony. She received the Nashville Songwriters Association's 'Songwriter/Artist Award' for the sixth consecutive year in 2013.

Also in 2013, aged just 23, Taylor was presented with the highest award in country music, the CMA 'Pinnacle Award'.

Taylor Swift performs onstage at the 54th Annual Grammy Awards held at Staples Center on February 12, 2012 in Los Angeles, California

Taylor Swift played the first of 13 North American stadium dates on The RED Tour at Ford Field in front of a sold-out crowd of more than 48,000 fans on May 4, 2013 in Detroit, Michigan

Red

Release date: October 2012 | Record label: Big Machine

TRACK LIST

1. State of Grace
2. Red
3. Treacherous
4. I Knew You Were Trouble
5. All Too Well
6. 22
7. I Almost Do
8. We Are Never Ever Getting Back Together
9. Stay Stay Stay
10. The Last Time
11. Holy Ground
12. Sad Beautiful Tragic
13. The Lucky One
14. Everything Has Changed (ft Ed Sheeran)
15. Starlight
16. Begin Again
17. The Moment I Knew
18. Come Back...Be Here
19. Girl At Home

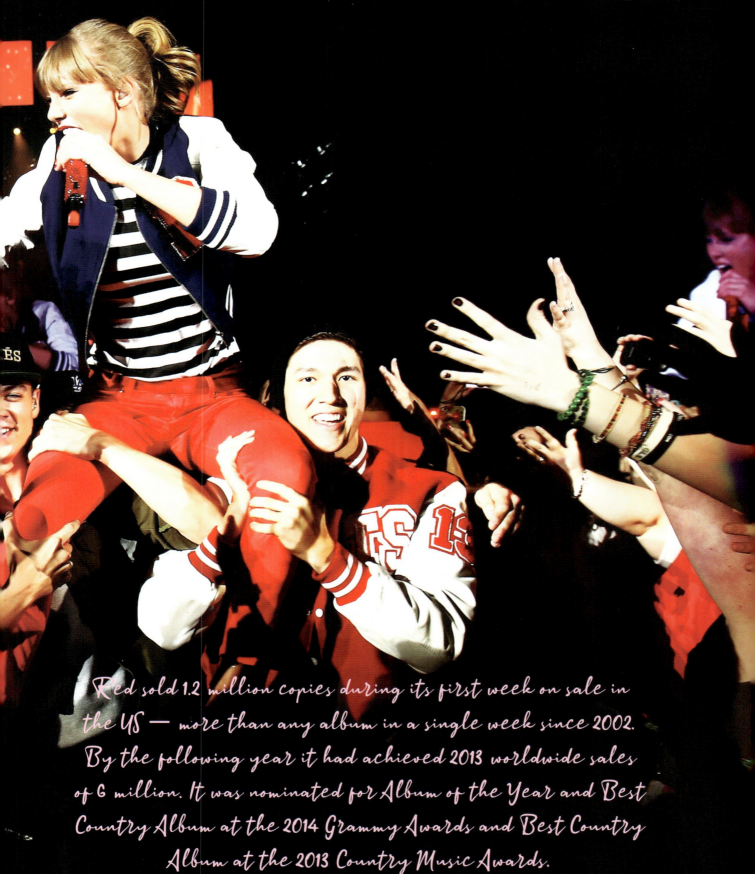

Red sold 1.2 million copies during its first week on sale in the US — more than any album in a single week since 2002. By the following year it had achieved 2013 worldwide sales of 6 million. It was nominated for Album of the Year and Best Country Album at the 2014 Grammy Awards and Best Country Album at the 2013 Country Music Awards.

Taylor Swift performs onstage during the 56th Grammy Awards at Staples Center on January 26, 2014 in Los Angeles, California

She had reached the top of the mountain as far as country music goes. And achieved her long-held ambition of winning a Grammy. What next?

European leg of her blockbuster *The Red Tour* show to Berlin's, O2 World playing to a capacity crowd of more than 10,700 fans on February 7, 2014 in Berlin, Germany

The 1989 era

Of course Taylor had a plan. Having achieved global fame as a country artist, she decided to reinvent herself completely as a mainstream pop star.

As she told *Rolling Stone* afterwards; 'I felt so proud and still feel so proud of my origins in Nashville. But at a certain point, I started to feel like, "Am I allowed to colour outside the lines here?" And it really was amazing, on *Red*, to realize, "Oh, I'm allowed in these rooms, I'm accepted in these rooms." That was something that freed me up for a world of change and challenge and innovation. I never would've had the bravery to make the full leap into pop music, if I hadn't been able to do what I did with *Red* and to work with the people that I worked with. I will always look back on it and think, "Wow, that was really the beginning of everything that I'm doing [now]".'

The only blot on the horizon was that Taylor's long honeymoon as the darling of the media began to tarnish. Other young, attractive, talented and hardworking stars have suffered similar backlashes, but it was particularly tough for Taylor who had always been fuelled by a need for approval, as she put it later, 'to be thought of as "good"'.

Things started harmlessly enough with some jokes about Taylor's love life, but quickly morphed into something less good-natured, characterising Taylor as a something of a mad girlfriend. *Billboard* had once described Taylor as constructing her songs like 'a Romeo-and-Juliet romantic who'll push you off the balcony if you betray her' and the idea of Taylor as this 'character' was now being developed throughout the media, fuelled by her run of highly publicised romances.

One headline even ran; 'Is Taylor Swift a psychopath'.

Although such scrutiny was hard to take, Taylor used it as more fodder for her writing …. And what she came up with next blew everything out of the water.

Her fifth album, titled 1989 after the year of her birth, was quite simply a pop masterpiece.

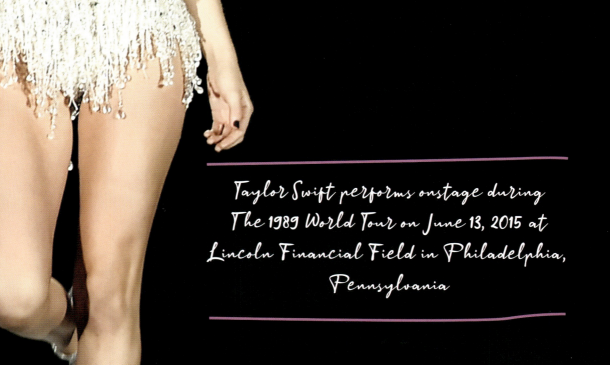

Taylor Swift performs onstage during The 1989 World Tour on June 13, 2015 at Lincoln Financial Field in Philadelphia, Pennsylvania

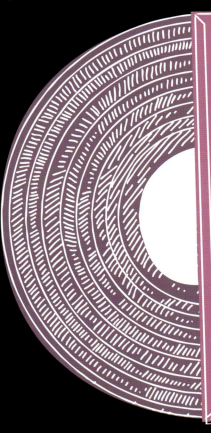

1989

Release date: October 2014 | Record label: Big Machine

TRACK LIST

1. Welcome to New York
2. Blank Space
3. Style
4. Out of the Woods
5. All You Had to Do Was Stay
6. Shake It Off
7. I Wish You Would
8. Bad Blood
9. Wildest Dreams
10. How You Get the Girl
11. This Love
12. I Know Places
13. Clean

Becoming Taylor's fourth American #1 album, 1989 topped the Billboard 200 chart for 11 weeks, becoming her third consecutive album to sell above one million copies in its first week — a new record for any artist. By going on to win Album of the Year at the 2016 Grammy's, 1989 made Taylor the first female artist ever to win the prize twice.

Taylor Swift performs live on stage during 'The 1989 World Tour' night 2 at Lanxess Arena on June 20, 2015 in Cologne, Germany

1989 also made clear that Taylor had shed her country roots completely; there was no marketing push in the country music media at all. The content was a very positive repost to the criticisms she had begun receiving about her personal life and relationship issues. Critics praised her songs for bringing emotional engagement into mainstream pop. The album appeared on several 2010s best albums lists and *Rolling Stone* featured it in their 2020 revised list of their 500 Greatest Albums of All Time.

Best of all of course, *1989* won Album of the Year and Best Pop Vocal Album at the 58th Grammy Awards in 2016.

But what Taylor did next brought further publicity and criticism, this time of her business decisions.

Taylor was now a powerhouse in the music industry, and of course, no longer a child star but a fully grown adult with views of her own. Thanks to her parents, she was completely business savvy and well able to stand up for herself, as she did by entering the debate about the growth of the new streaming services.

At that time, the whole landscape of the music industry was changing fast as digital downloads and streaming came in and physical album sales were in decline.

Taylor felt she needed to take a stand over her rights as an artist. 'I'm not willing to contribute my life's work to an experiment that I don't feel fairly compensates the

Madonna & Taylor Swift during the 2015 iHeartRadio Music Awards, live on NBC from The Shrine Auditorium on March 29, 2015, Los Angeles, California

writers, producers, artists, and creators of this music," she said.

The first hint of her views on the digital landscape came in an article she wrote for the *Wall Street Journal* in July 2014 headlined, 'For Taylor Swift, the Future of Music Is a Love Story'. Overall a positive piece about the music industry, the article also included a section on Taylor's belief that 'music should be paid for'.

'Music is art, and art is important and rare. Important, rare things are valuable. Valuable things should be paid for. It's my opinion that music should not be free, and my prediction is that individual artists and their labels will someday decide what an album's price point is. I hope they don't underestimate themselves or undervalue their art.'

Then she refused to allow 1989 to go on the leading streaming service Spotify saying it was wrong to, in effect, give away her album for free and that their service was damaging the songwriters' royalties system. She also withdrew her entire back catalogue.

The following year she challenged the massive and influential Apple Music organisation, persuading them to change their business model by withholding her 1989 album from their music platform until they agreed to reverse their payment policy of not giving the artists royalties during the three-month trial period.

By speaking out against the idea of giving music away for free and controlling access

Squad girls

Taylor has lots of famous girlfriends who are known in the press as members of her 'squad'. Some of these women featured in Taylor's iconic video for Bad Blood and Taylor also wore a squad shirt in the video for *Look What You Made Me Do*.

Squad members old and new, many of them actresses and models include:

Selena Gomez

Martha Hunt

Abigail Anderson Lucier

Gigi Hadid

Karlie Kloss

Carla Delevingne

Blake Lively

Hailee Steinfeld

Emma Stone

Lena Dunham

Lily Aldridge

to her material by streaming services, Taylor helped shape how the new world of digital music works. After making her views known, she re-added her catalogue, plus 1989, to Spotify and other digital streaming platforms in 2017.

Through all of that, she was planning her 1989 world tour which ran from May to December 2015, comprising a record-breaking run of 85 shows that saw Taylor playing to a total of over 2.2 million fans making it the best attended tour of all time. It was also the highest grossing of that year and then the entire decade, bringing in over US$199.4 million in North America alone, smashing the previous all-time high of $162 million set by the Rolling Stones 10 years before.

Taking in North America, Europe, Japan and Oceania, the tour was extended to include dates in Singapore and China.

As always, Taylor was closely involved with the planning and design of her tour which was seven months in conception and three months in rehearsal. It was a challenge for Taylor and her team to create the intimate experience she wanted for her fans, while needing to perform in huge stadiums to accommodate them.

Her set was predominantly of songs from *1989*, but she also included songs from her back catalogue. Many of the shows featured special guests including members of her 'squad'.

Reviews for the tour were spectacular, with critics agreeing she had pushed the production and her own performance beyond anything seen before, to give fans the best night of their lives.

The *New York Times'* review of the show said,' Though her lyrics have gradually begun to acknowledge the sensual, she remains effectively chaste onstage, even when flanked by shirtless dancers on "I Knew You Were Trouble." But her between-song chatter, always inspirational, now carries the weight of experience. "You are not damaged goods just because you've made mistakes," she said. "You are not someone else's opinion of you."' Yet the headlines were getting to her.

After the 1989 world tour she knew she needed a break. Although as she put it, 'People might need a break' [from her].

So, now the biggest pop star on the planet, she dropped off the radar.

Stellar singles

Shake it off

Calling out all her haters — this was Taylor's catchy retort that she would continue her success without caring what her detractors thought.

This single was #1 in the US and #2 in the UK where it remains her best-selling ever. It stayed at number one on the American charts for four weeks and then remained on the chart in various positions for 50 weeks in total. It went on to receive diamond certification, three Grammy nominations and won a People's Choice Award.

Blank space

This single cemented Taylor's shift to the mainstream and acknowledged her new image that was surfacing because she was becoming known for writing about her exes. Taylor told *Rolling Stone* that *Blank Space* was written as a satire on her perceived image saying she thought, 'OK, this is what you're all saying about me. Let me just write from this character for a second'.

The single picked up three Grammy nominations. The song not only reached number one on Billboard Hot 100 but stayed there for seven weeks. The music video for this song depicted Taylor as a crazed woman — a potential parody of her portrayal in the media — and won for Best Pop Video at the 2015 MTV Awards.

Bad Blood

This hit song about betrayal peaked at number one on the Billboard Hot 100. It also reached the top spot in Australia, New Zealand and Canada. This song won the Grammy for Best Music Video, which featured cameos from stars in Taylor's 'squad' including Selena Gomez, Hailee Steinfeld, Gigi Hadid, Cara Delevingne and Zendaya.

Taylor Swift performs during "The 1989 World Tour" at Levi's Stadium on August 15, 2015 in Santa Clara, California

The 1989 World Tour Live In Los Angeles at
Staples Center on August 22, 2015

The Reputation era

I t was probably to be expected that after such incredible success the media would start to turn against Taylor. She was under intense scrutiny at every turn and all her actions and decisions were analysed as the media questioned what was 'real' and what was for publicity purposes'. Was she really friends with the models and actresses in her 'squad'? Was she really the 'victim' in these feuds with Kanye West and Kim Kardashian? Did she take on streaming services purely to increase her album sales? She was in the gossip columns as much as the music pages.

Having stepped off social media during her hiatus, one of Taylor's rare public comments on her situation came at the 2016 Grammy Awards when *1989* won for Album of the Year. As she accepted her prize she said 'I want to say to all the young women out there -- there are going to be people along the way who will try to undercut your success or take credit for your accomplishments or your fame. But if you just focus on the work and you don't let those people side-track you, someday when you get where you are going, you will look around and you will know that it was you and the people who love you who put you there'.

She was taking her own advice and focusing on her next album, *Reputation*, writing to re-set herself. She took inspiration from her tempestuous relationship with the media and the personal difficulties involved in navigating a love life against such a background and has since described the album as being 'cathartic'.

Working with producers Jack Antonoff, Max Martin and Shellback again, she built her new album around darker electropop sounds, using synthesisers and manipulated vocals amid other techniques.

Fans had a long wait for this new music — but it was definitely worth it.

Taylor Swift onstage at the Z100's Jingle Ball 2017, December 8, 2017 in New York City

Reputation

Release date: November 2017 | Record label: Big Machine

TRACK LIST

1. Ready for It?
2. End Game (ft Ed Sheeran and Future)
3. I Did Something Bad
4. Don't Blame Me
5. Delicate
6. Look What You Made Me Do
7. So It Goes
8. Gorgeous
9. Getaway Car
10. King of My Heart
11. Dancing with Our Hands Tied
12. Dress
13. This Is Why We Can't Have Nice Things
14. Call It What You Want
15. New Year's Day

Reputation became Taylor's fourth consecutive album to enter the American charts straight in at #1, where it remained for four weeks. First-week sales were over 1.2 million copies, making Taylor the first artist to have four consecutive albums sell over a million in the first week of release. The album also topped the charts in the UK, Canada and Australia. By the end of 2017 *Reputation* had sold over 4.5 million copies and become the world's best-selling album by a female artist.

In keeping with the mood of the album, Taylor did not do any press interviews to promote it. Nevertheless it topped the charts for three weeks, becoming her fifth number one hit on the US Billboard Hot 100 and also gained the most plays on Spotify in a single day. Reputation became the top-selling US album of the year.

By the time her Reputation tour kicked off Taylor only had her own records to beat — which she did, topping the gross and attendance figures set by the 1989 tour in a series of 53 all stadium shows which ran from May to November 2018.

Taylor Swift onstage during Taylor Swift reputation Stadium Tour at Levi's Stadium on May 11, 2018 in Santa Clara, California

Taylor Swift performs onstage during the 2018 Reputation Stadium Tour at Soldier Field on June 1, 2018 in Chicago, Illinois

The reviews raved about the shows, which combined Broadway theatricality with Gothic visuals and costumes, describing the tour as Taylor's best ever. Again she managed to retain a strong connection with her fans despite the huge stage and skyscraper set she commanded.

In North America alone, her Reputation tour grossed $202.3 million, breaking her own record for the highest-grossing tour by a female artist on that continent, previously held by the 1989 World Tour, despite performing fewer dates. 2.55 million people across the planet saw her play.

Her live shows had got more and more elaborate. Having started simply as a girl with a guitar, the production values of Taylor's performances were now off the scale including light shows, pyrotechnics, more dancers and costume changes and even incorporating some risqué moves. Everything was seamless.

Once again she had set the bar stratospherically high. The only records and standards left to beat were her own.

Moving on

Reputation was the final record Taylor made with Big Machine. After 12 years her contract had expired and in late 2018 she signed with Republic records, part of the Universal Music group. While it was undoubtedly a multi-million-dollar deal, Taylor made the move as much for her rights as the money. The new contract agreed that she would own her own masters going forward.

However, her first six albums would still be controlled by Big Machine. Although she said that she had 'made peace with the fact that eventually [Borchetta] would sell them' she was very upset when he had decided to sell them to Scooter Braun, a talent manager whose clients had included Kanye West, and who she felt had bullied her in the past.

Taylor was completely against the deal, claiming that Borchetta had rejected her earlier attempts to acquire the master tapes herself.

She further alleged that Scott Borchetta knew of her feelings toward Scooter Braun and through the sale of her masters both men were complicit in 'controlling a woman who didn't want to be associated with them. In perpetuity.'

But she was unable to negotiate a deal with Braun and in turn he sold her back catalogue to a private investment firm in 2020.

So Taylor decided that she would regain artistic and financial control of her old music by re-recording new versions of those albums. In this way she hoped that her new versions, rather than the originals, would be used in future licensing deals and preferred by fans. As she said at the time, 'Artists deserve to own their work. I just feel very passionately about that.'

Her August 2019 album Lover was the first that she would 'own' and became that year's best-selling album by a solo artist. Taylor described the album as 'a love letter to love itself'.

Onstage at the 2019 American Music Awards at the Microsoft Theater, November 24, 2019, Los Angeles, California

Lover

Release date: August 2019 | Record label: Republic

TRACK LIST

1. I Forgot That You Existed
2. Cruel Summer
3. Lover
4. The Man
5. Archer
6. I Think He Knows
7. Miss Americana & The Heartbreak Prince
8. Paper Rings
9. Cornelia Street
10. Death by a Thousand Cuts
11. London Boy
12. Soon You'll Get Better
13. False God
14. You Need to Calm Down
15. Afterglow
16. Me!
17. It's Nice to Have a Friend
18. Daylight

The release was heralded by two singles, *Me!* and *You Need to Calm Down*, which both reached number two on the Hot 100 and helped get the album to number one. The album was Grammy-nominated for best pop vocal album, while *You Need to Calm Down* was nominated for best pop solo performance and the track *Lover* was nominated for song of the year. But none of them picked up a prize on the night — something that Taylor was seen to be disappointed about during her Miss Americana documentary, saying, 'If I don't beat anything I've done prior, it's a failure'. Yet Lover was far from a failure, providing Taylor with her sixth #1 album in the US and going on to top the charts in the UK, Australia, Canada, Mexico, Norway, Sweden, and several others. Sales of 3.2 million copies in 2019, made *Lover* the best-selling studio album of the year and gave Taylor the accolade of being the best-selling musician in the world for 2019.

Her comment in the documentary showed exactly the high standards that Taylor sets herself. Most critics reviewed *Lover* positively, praising its emotional honesty and free-spirited style. Pitchfork music site's review called it 'bright and fun'.

But plans to promote the album any further had to be cancelled because of the Covid-19 pandemic which put a stop to all festivals and concert tours in 2020 including Taylor's planned sixth tour, Lover Fest scheduled to begin on 5 April that year.

Forced to scrap her plans, Taylor had to stay at home like everyone else. But she used her time wisely, appearing to revel in the unexpected period of uninterrupted creative and writing time.

Having ended 2019 by winning the first ever Billboard Woman of the Decade Award for being 'one of the most accomplished musical artists of all time over the course of the 2010s', Taylor turned her enforced quarantine into an opportunity to build on that achievement.

She conceived and produced another stand-out album *Folklore,* which took her fans completely by surprise.

Taylor Swift attends the InStyle And Warner Bros. Golden Globes After Party 2019 at The Beverly Hilton Hotel on January 6, 2019 in Beverly Hills, California

Arriving for Billboard's 2019 Woman of the Year at the Hollywood Palladium in Los Angeles on December 12, 2019

Fun fact

'Number one for me, most influential factor in my life is cats," says Taylor. 'I have cats. I'm obsessed with them. They're just a real joy to live with. I love my cats so much'. She has even trademarked the names of her cats, Meredith Grey, Olivia Benson and new kitten Benjamin Button for future merchandise opportunities including clothing, phone accessories, toys, luggage, home furnishings, key rings, arts and crafts kits, glassware, ornaments, and colouring books.

Taylor Swift performs onstage during the 2019 American Music Awards at Microsoft Theater on November 24, 2019 in Los Angeles, California

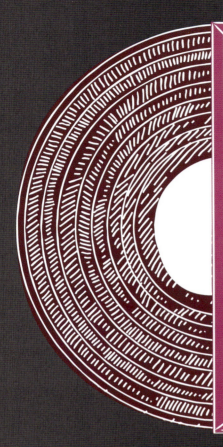

Folklore

Release date: July 2020 | Record label: Republic

TRACK LIST

1. The 1
2. Cardigan
3. The Last Great American Dynasty
4. Exile (Ft Bon Iver)
5. My Tears Ricochet
6. Mirrorball
7. Seven
8. August
9. This Is Me Trying
10. Illicit Affairs
11. Invisible String
12. Mad woman
13. Epiphany
14. Betty
15. Peace
16. Hoax
17. The Lakes

Grammy award-winning *Folklore* spent eight weeks at number 1 on the Billboard 200 and became the best-selling album in the United States in 2020. This gave Taylor yet another 'record' as the first artist to have the best-selling album of a calendar year five times thanks to the earlier successes of *Fearless* in 2009, *1989* in 2014, *Reputation* in 2017, and *Lover* in 2019.

In stark contrast to most of her recent output, Folklore, her eighth album, was released without fanfare because, as she put it, the strange events and enforced isolation caused by the pandemic had shown her that 'nothing is guaranteed'.

The album is a mellow double, with 17 fresh and truthful tracks, less showy than much of her previous, more pop-centred, output. It has a Cottage core vibe that romanticizes escaping the noisy modern life to return to a simpler time.

She collaborated with Justin Vernon from Bon Iver and Aaron Dessner from The National to produce this indie, electro-folk, alternative rock offering, driven by guitar and piano all beautifully produced and arranged to provide a laidback reflective vibe.

Stripped back and understated, many critics felt it could be her landmark album. Further validation, were it needed, came when Folklore picked up the Grammy for Album of the Year in 2021, giving Taylor a record-breaking third win in this category.

Key among its tracks was *The Last Great American Dynasty,* which showed that Taylor's fantastic storytelling abilities were undiminished as she incorporated historical detail and American imagery into this tale of women's treatment by society. *Mirrorball,* a dreamy take on fame, and the anthemic *August* were other standout songs.

A strong element counting towards the success of this new work was that Taylor was in such a good place personally. Now in a happy, long-term relationship with English actor Joe Alwyn she didn't have any real-life trauma to mine for content and so was able to avoid further media scrutiny by imagining characters and their emotions instead of using her own experiences.

As she said in an interview at the time, continuing to write diaristic music was unsustainable, and like 'loading a cannon of clickbait when that's not what I want for my life'.

Referencing Joe in her Grammy acceptance speech, Taylor said that he was the first person that she played every single song that she writes, adding, 'I had the best time writing songs with you in quarantine'.

Although Taylor keeps her relationship with Joe very private she has spoken about how their time together in lockdown meant that they began to write together, something that otherwise would probably not have happened. It's since been revealed that Joe has credits on Folklore under the pseudonym of William Bowery for the tracks *Betty* and *Exile*.

Stellar Single

Cardigan

A song that stole the show when it came to its music video Cardigan — released as the lead single from the album. It was rumoured to be about embracing the cottage/fairy aesthetic in both sound and music video. Not only did this song debut at the number one spot on the Billboard Hot 100, but the album itself landed at number one on the Billboard 200. The song was also nominated for two Grammys, with the album *Folklore* winning for Album of the Year.

Taylor then surprised fans again by releasing a second album, *Evermore*, described as a 'sister' to *Folklore*, only a few months later at Christmas 2020, just before her 31st birthday.

She tweeted to fans that ever since she was 13, she had been excited about turning 31 because it was her lucky number backwards and that is why she wanted to surprise her fans with this album now. She said it was also a present from her to her fans as a thank you for the fact that they had always been so caring, thoughtful and supportive on all her birthdays.

Evermore

Release date: December 2020 | Record label: Republic

TRACK LIST

1. Willow
2. Champagne Problems
3. Gold Rush
4. 'Tis The Damn Season
5. Tolerate It
6. No Body, No Crime (feat Haim)
7. Happiness
8. Dorothea
9. Coney Island (feat The National)
10. Ivy
11. Cowboy Like Me
12. Long Story Short
13. Marjorie
14. Closure
15. Evermore (Bon Iver)

The album reached number one in the US, becoming Taylor's eighth consecutive Billboard 200 #1 debut, and staying at number one for four weeks. It also topped the charts in the UK and around the world, selling more than one million copies globally in its first week.

Like *Folklore* before it, *Evermore* was acclaimed for its nuanced storytelling and as being another introspective and restrained piece of work. Again it was inspired by escapism and romanticism and explored an imaginary world and fictional narratives. Joe Alwyn as William Bowery has co-writing credits on the title track, plus *Champagne Problems* and *Coney Island*.

Commentators say that Taylor and Joe got closer than ever during lockdown when, as well as dealing with the restrictions imposed by the pandemic, Taylor was also coping with her mother Andrea's ill health as she battled cancer.

Evermore was listed by various publications in their year-end rankings of the best albums of 2020 and received a nominated for Album of the Year at the 2022, 64th Grammy awards.

Performing at the 55th Academy of Country Music Awards at the Grand Ole Opry in Nashville, Tennessee.

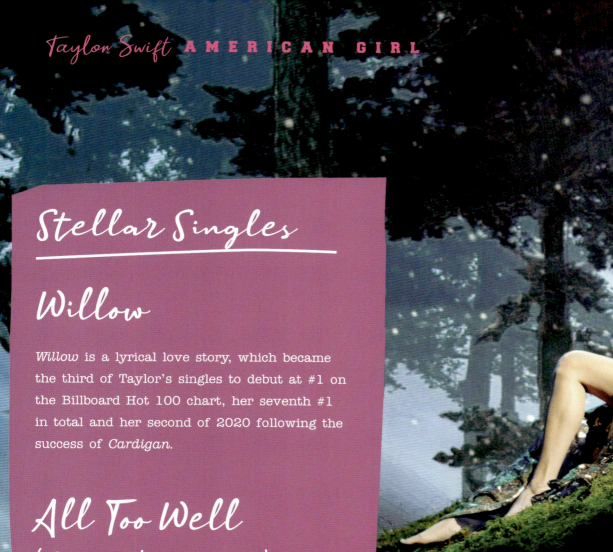

Stellar Singles

Willow

Willow is a lyrical love story, which became the third of Taylor's singles to debut at #1 on the Billboard Hot 100 chart, her seventh #1 in total and her second of 2020 following the success of *Cardigan*.

All Too Well
(10-minute version)

Issued following the release of *Red — Taylor's Version*, this song, thought to be about Jake Gyllenhaal, was originally long but cut back for the original album. Now released at its original length, it has gained cult status as the longest song to make #1 on the charts, beating the record held for 50 years by Don McLean's American Pie which was 8.42 minutes.

Performing at the 63rd Annual Grammy
Awards broadcast on March 14, 2021

In 2021 Taylor began releasing her re-recorded back catalogue, beginning with *Fearless (Taylor's Version)* in April and *Red (Taylor's Version)* in November

Fearless (Taylor's Version) became the first re-recorded album to top the *Billboard* 200 and following the success of sister albums *Folklore* and *Evermore* made Taylor the first female artist to have three number-one albums in under a year.

Taylor then clocked up her eighth chart topping album when *Red (Taylor's Version)* then also went to number one, breaking the record for the largest vinyl sales week for an album in the history of music sales data — with unit sales totalling 105,000 — and beating the record set by *Evermore* mere months previously.

Gorgeous

As one of the most scrutinised women in the world, Taylor's fashion choices supply endless column inches and fan debate.

Like all enduring pop stars, Taylor changes up her looks to match her current music and vibe. Since her early days when she embraced the country music style of cowboy boots, denim and flouncy dresses, fans have seen her go through various regenerations including the signature red lips and 'cat eyes' of her *Red*-era, her short sparkly flapper-style dresses for 1989, the high-waisted shorts and leather looks of *Reputation* and the pastel palette of *Lover* days.

Most recently, to chime with the indie-folk influences on Folklore and Evermore, Taylor has introduced her fans to the style of 'cottage core' by wearing oversized lace dresses, knitted cardigans and denim jackets.

She's tall, fierce and beautiful enough to hold her own whenever she has appeared at Victoria's Secret fashion shows, where she has rocked some incredible looks.

She is also blessed with perfect hair which she's famous for flicking about in her shows She doesn't want any damage from hair dye so leaves her colour natural — unlike many pop stars who appear with their hair all colours of the rainbow. Taylor prefers to experiment with styles and cuts instead. The long, naturally curly hair of her early fame has variously been replaced with sharper, sleek bobs long and short and mid-length beach-waved looks.

If this was a movie

Taylor occasional forays into the acting profession include:

Valentine's Day

Taylor played high school student Felicia Miller who was in a relationship with first love Willy, played by Taylor Lautner, in this 2010 film about a group of related characters and their struggles with love.

The Giver

Taylor took the cameo role of Rosemary in this 2014 film adaptation of Lois Lowry's dystopian novel for young readers.

Cats

Taylor played Bombalurina in the 2019 film adaptation of Andrew Lloyd Webber's stage musical *Cats*, singing the song *Macavity*

Miss Americana

Taylor is centre stage in this documentary about her life and career, called *Miss Americana*.

Netflix and chill

TV

When Taylor has a cosy night in she loves to settle down in front of the television. Her favourite shows are:

Grey's Anatomy

Fleabag

Killing Eve

Game of Thrones

Queer Eye

At the movies

Taylor has said in many interviews that her overall favourite film is the Christmas rom com *Love Actually*.

She's also a big fan of the break-up movie, *Something Great*

At the ... Alice
Tully ... December 16,
... City

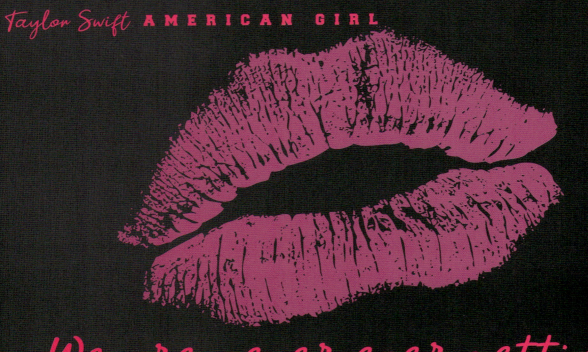

We are never ever getting back together...

Taylor's love life is of endless fascination to the press, not least because she became known for writing 'break up tracks' about her previous relationships.

From the days of her first hit *Tim McGraw*, rumoured to be about teenage boyfriend Brandon Borello, she has used her experiences of romance and heartbreak in her music. Explaining how she can draw inspiration from anything — a memory or even a glance — Taylor gave *The Washington Post* some further insight as to how she worked, saying 'If you're a good storyteller you can take a dirty look somebody gives you, or if a guy you used to have flirtations with starts dating a new girl, or somebody you're casually talking to says something that makes you so mad — you can create a scenario around that'.

Her method does clarify why some men have been amazed to hear that their very brief interaction with Taylor has apparently made it to a song. Evidently Taylor can make a little information go a long way. For example in the song Enchanted, which is about infatuation with someone from a first meeting and wondering if the feeling will be reciprocated when Taylor softly pleads, 'Please don't be in love with someone else', was reputedly inspired by a brief conversation with musician Adam Young.

But obviously her best inspiration of all comes from her real love affairs. Here's a quick rundown of her most public relationships.

Joe Jonas

One of Taylor's most famous exes is singer and actor Joe Jonas of The Jonas Brothers. The couple dated in 2008 when they were 18 and Taylor spoke afterwards about the upset she suffered when they finished — announcing during a TV interview with US host Ellen DeGeneres just afterwards that Joe had broken up with her over the phone in a 27- second call. Her sarcastically titled track *Forever and Always* was written about Joe. Now years down the line, Taylor and Joe have cleared the air and are friends again. Taylor even apologised for throwing shade at him back then.

'It did feel nice," Jonas said of her apology. 'It's something that I was probably feeling pretty bad about when I was younger, but, at the end of the day, I've moved on. I'm sure Taylor's moved on. It feels nice. We're all friends. It's all good. We were so young.'

John Mayer

Taylor was just 19 when she began a relationship with fellow singer/songwriter John Mayer, who was 32 years at the time. The couple dated for just under a year and following their break-up — one of Taylor's firsts– she wrote the track *Dear John*, which reportedly left him 'humiliated'. Its lyrics include the lines, 'Don't you think nineteen's too young to be played by your dark, twisted games?' and 'All the girls that you've run dry/Have tired, lifeless eyes because you burned them out/But I took your matches before fire could catch me/So don't look now/I'm shining like fireworks /Over your sad empty town.'

There were other tracks too — *Ours, Superman, The Story of Us* and *Half of My Heart*, have all been mentioned as relating to John Meyer.

Taylor Lautner

Taylor and Taylor? It had to happen. Pop princess Taylor Swift met actor Taylor Lautner when they both appeared in the film *Valentine's Day* in 2009, coincidentally playing girlfriend and boyfriend, and they went on to date for some three months. The track *Back to December* from Taylor's 2010 album *Speak Now* is reportedly about that relationship. She sings of a guy with 'tan skin and a sweet smile' who she left in exchange for 'freedom'.

Corey Monteith

Taylor's track *Mine* on *Speak Now* is rumoured to be about actor Corey Monteith, who played Finn Hudson in *Glee*. The pair are thought to have dated for a month in Spring 2010. Following Corey's sudden death in 2013 Taylor tweeted that she was 'speechless'.

Jake Gyllenhaal

Taylor dated actor Jake Gyllenhaal, 10 years her senior, for a couple of months at the end of 2010 before calling it a day in January 2011. Many of the songs on Taylor's next album *Red* were thought to be based on him, including *The Moment I Knew*, rumoured to be about the time he didn't show up at her 21st birthday party, *We Are Never Ever Getting Back Together,* and *All Too Well*.

The track *Begin Again* on the *Red* album is supposedly about moving on from Jake with Conor Kennedy.

Conor Kennedy

Taylor's fascination with the American Kennedy family is well-known, so she surely couldn't pass on a chance to date a real member of that dynasty — Conor Kennedy, a great-nephew of assassinated US President JFK. This time Taylor was the elder in the relationship — 22 to Conor's 18 years — but the whole thing was short-lived, a summer romance which was all over by October 2012.

Harry Styles

When two of the biggest music stars on the planet get together there's bound to be a lot of interest. So it was hashtag '#Haylor' when fans got wind of a relationship between Taylor and boyband megastar Harry Styles from One Direction in 2012.

Although their time together was short — and is rumoured to have ended with a big row during a New Year's holiday on the British Virgin Islands — fans got a lot out of it. Both Taylor and Harry subsequently released music believed to be about their time together.

Several of Taylor's tracks have been mentioned as possible Harry-related songs, including *I knew You Were Trouble*, *I Wish You Would*, *Style* and *Out of the Woods*.

For his part Harry co-wrote the 2015 One Direction hit *Perfect* on the *Made in the A.M.* album which was thought to be about Taylor and included the lyric, 'And if you're looking for someone to write your break-up songs about, baby I'm perfect'. More recently *Two Ghosts* on his *Fine Line* album included a description of a woman with 'Same lips red, same eyes blue' which got fans wondering if this was also a reference to Taylor.

Calvin Harris

Taylor dated Scottish DJ and record producer Calvin Harris for over a year in 2015/16– that's a long relationship in Taylor-time — after the pair connected a the Brit Awards. The affair ended with the couple sayi they had 'different visions of their future'.

Songs rumoured to be about Calvin are *I Did Something Bad* and *Getaway Car* on Taylor's album *Reputation*.

Tom Hiddleston

When Taylor had a whirlwind romance with British actor Tom Hiddleston, famous as Marvel villain Loki, for a few months during the summer of 2016, it caused a huge media storm. Photographs of them partying in the States, the UK, Italy and Australia, and of Tom wearing a 'I Like TS' t-shirt, filled the gossip columns. When it ended Taylor wrote *Getaway Car* for her 2017 album *Reputation* which explains that the romance began too quickly after the end of another to really work — apparently referencing her move from Calvin Harris to Tom.

Joe Alwyn

Since May 2017, Taylor has been dating British actor Joe Alwyn who she met at the Met Gala in New York.

Spending quarantine together has reportedly brought the couple closer than ever — even to the extent of buying a townhouse together in London in 2021.

Joe has even begun to get involved with Taylor's music and has writing and co-production credits on her 2020 'quarantine albums' *Folklore* and *Evermore*.

A place in this world

Taylor recognises that she is a role model to young women and it's a responsibility that she takes seriously.

From her earliest days back in Nashville, Taylor has been famous for being accessible to her fans, the 'Swifties'. Taylor knows that many fans see her as being almost like an elder sister and so she has tried to stay as personally connected to them as possible. Right back when she was a teenager she set up a direct link with them through her *MySpace* page and by personally blogging.

She has always made a point of getting as up close and personal with fans as is possible, before, during and after shows, signing autographs, handing out hugs, throwing bracelets from the stage. Speaking in her 2021 autobiographical documentary *Miss Americana* she said of her fans, 'We feel like we grew up together...it's like they've been reading my diary.'

Swiftmas

Taylor delighted a group of her super fans in 2014 by sending them Christmas presents she had personally chosen and wrapped. While most arrived via FEDEX, Taylor delivered some of them in person.

Swiftmas, as the event became known, caused huge excitement throughout the Swiftie community and a video showing fan reactions to their gifts and visits received 1m views on YouTube in a week.

She's inventive about her fan interactions, for example when she hosted a top-secret fan streaming session for her 1989 album.

Swifties' social media accounts include varied examples of her generosity towards them, likening her to a fairy godmother as she does everything from visit them in hospital to helping pay off their college tuition fees.

But despite sharing so much with her fans over the years, Taylor had chosen to keep quiet about her personal and political views. From her early days as a very young star, she had always had a genuinely wholesome, entirely non-threatening image and never sought out controversy. She and her team were always acutely aware of the value of her 'brand' which made her an attractive proposition for advertisers and earned her royalties on merchandise and endorsement deals with companies including Diet Coke, Keds and Cover Girl.

As Taylor grew up she began to struggle with the advice she'd been given about keeping her personal opinions to herself. She realised that she could use her platform to further those topics about which she cared the most.

The first signs that she was preparing to get more involved in public debate came when she took on the streaming services in the mid-2010s.

Then Taylor really seemed to get into her stride following the David Mueller civil court case in 2017. Mueller was working as a DJ when he had met Taylor and maintained that she had ruined his career by falsely claiming he had sexually groped her back in 2013. Having always maintained that the assault had happened, Taylor was understandably keen to defend herself and so she countersued, asking for just $1 in compensation as she wanted to make a point, not money. She won her case and felt emboldened to help other victims, vowing to support organisations which help sexual assault victims defend themselves.

Now Taylor is sure to lend her voice to criticizing sexism and misogyny, signing up to support the Times Up Movement, aimed at addressing harassment, and making donations to the Rape, Abuse & Incest National Network as part of Sexual Assault Awareness Month.

With, as she described it, the 'masking tape' off her mouth, Taylor began making other personal statements, like for example encouraging her fans to register to vote by speaking out about the Nashville elections in 2018. Proving that her fans take a lot from her public statements as well as her music, voting registrations went up by 160,000 in just 48 hours when she declared her support for the Democratic party candidates. Now she actively uses her platform to shed light on social issues. In an interview with Vanity Fair, Taylor explained, 'The Trump presidency forced me to lean in and educate myself. I found myself talking about government and the presidency and policy with my boyfriend [actor Joe

Alwyn], who supported me in speaking out," she said.

"I started talking to my family and friends about politics and learning as much as I could about where I stand. I'm proud to have moved past fear and self-doubt, and to endorse and support leadership that moves us beyond this divisive, heart-breaking moment in time."

Taylor has made numerous personal donations to charity, recorded songs to raise money for various causes, and lent her voice to different movements including speaking out against LGBTQ discrimination, police brutality, white supremacy, and racism.

Taylor Swift accepting the Gracies Grand Award, via video link at the 46th Annual Gracie Awards on October 26, 2021

Taylor Swift AMERICAN GIRL

Recognition

Taylor has won so many awards in her career that there are memes of her 'pretending to be shocked' face.

Her prize haul includes:

11 Grammy awards including three for Album of the Year
1 Emmy Award
34 American Music Awards (most for any artist)
55 Guinness World Records
8 Academy of Country Music Awards
25 US Billboard Music Awards
2 BRIT Awards

Other accolades include featuring on:-

Rolling Stone magazine's list of 100 Greatest Songwriters of All Time (2015)
Billboard's Greatest of All Time Artists list (2019)
Billboard's Woman of the 2010s Decade
American Music Awards Artist of the 2010s Decade

Attending the "All Too Well" premiere at AMC Lincoln Square, November 12, 2021, New York

Commentators have speculated that Taylor is so influential that she could one day successfully run for political office herself — she has 200 million followers (and counting) on Instagram. But it's more likely that she'll stay in the music business. Speaking to New York Magazine back in 2013 she guessed that 'When I'm 40 and nobody wants to see me in a sparkly dress anymore I'll be like "Cool, I'll just go in the studio and write songs for kids". It's looking like a good pension plan'.

But now with almost 10 years of further success under her belt, and recently greeted with fresh critical acclaim for her new Americana-style work, she's probably reconsidering that idea. The Queen of Pandemic Productivity shows no signs of slowing down …

"I never want to get to the point where success and nominations and things like that ever seem just like something that happens every day,"

Taylor Swift